The Cosmos Is Alive

The Cosmos Is Alive

Poems by

Keith Gaboury

© 2023 Keith Gaboury. All rights reserved.
This material may not be reproduced in any form, published,
reprinted, recorded, performed, broadcast,
rewritten or redistributed without
the explicit permission of Keith Gaboury.
All such actions are strictly prohibited by law.

Cover image by Fabrice Villard,
Author photo by Jacob Gaboury
Cover design by Shay Culligan

ISBN: 978-1-63980-422-1

Kelsay Books
502 South 1040 East, A-119
American Fork, Utah 84003
Kelsaybooks.com

The following poems are dedicated to my family.
I love you like the stars love the sky.

Acknowledgments

Grateful acknowledgements are made to the following publications in which these poems (in some cases, earlier versions with different titles) originally appeared.

Abstract: Contemporary Expressions: "Mary's Moonbeams," "The Moon Water Trip," "The Apollo National Park," "NASA Spacesuit Test," "Lunar Trash Mission #7"
After Happy Hour Review: "The Planetary Invaders Recovery Group"
Bacopa Literary Review: "The Cherry Blossom Planet"
Bay Area Generations: "Survival," "Plasma Twister"
The Birds We Piled Loosely: "An Astronaut's Daughter Speaks," "The Cosmos Is Alive," "Wild," "Morning News in the Twenty-Second Century"
Boston Poetry Magazine: "The Moon Tree in Central Park," "Moon Rocks at Large"
Crab Fat Magazine: "My Heartland Moonbeams"
The Ear: "I Walk into Your Galaxy"
Hello Universe Lovers: "Ancient Battle in the Nile," "Space Vision," "An Astronaut's Daughter Speaks," "The Milky Way in L.A.," "My Heartland Moonbeams," "Wild," "Blood in the Cosmos," "Planet X Soap Opera," "The Cosmos Is Alive," "Morning News in the Twenty-Second Century," "Lunar Kingdom," "Plasma Twister," "The Moon Country Museum & Bar," "Jacob as Asteroid Miner," "Dear Outer Space," "The Apollo National Park," "My Caridocentric Sister," "Project Echo," "Laika," "NASA Spacesuit Test," "Look Up," "I Walk Into Your Galaxy," "Lunar Trash Mission #7," "Hello Urban Universe"
Eclectica Magazine: "Space Vision," "Ancient Battle in the Nile"
Five 2 One Magazine: "Rejoice in Caffeinated Spin"
Flypaper Magazine: "My Caridocentric Sister"
Fredericksburg Literary Art & Review: "Laika"
Literary Juice: "Jacob as Asteroid Miner"

Map Literary: "Planet X Soap Opera"
The 40th *New Millennium Writings* Poetry Contest: "The Milky Way in L.A." (Honorable Mention)
Oddball Magazine: "Gecko Sex in Space"
Passaic / Völuspá: "Blood in the Cosmos," "My Steampunked Universe"
Permafrost Magazine: "Dear Outer Space,"
Poetry Quarterly: "Ancient Battle in the Nile," "Project Echo" (2017 Rebecca Lard Award Finalist)

Contents

Dear astronaut in training,	13
The year before I left for Mars,	15
The cherry blossom planet	17
My heartland moonbeams	18
The cosmos is alive	19
Are we alone?	21
Native	22
I carry wonder	23
Look up	24
The Milky Way in L.A.	25
My steampunked universe	26
My punked erasure	27
Ancient battle in the Nile	30
Space vision	31
Laika	32
Enos and Ham	33
Edwin's body	35
Edwin's erasure	36
Project Echo	37
Planet X soap opera	38
Survival	40
NASA spacesuit test	41
Pluto Time	42
The Apollo National Park	44
Lunar Trash Mission #7	45
Family land	47
Left to scream	48
Moon rocks at large	50
My cardiocentric sister	51
Mary's moonbeams	52
Lunar Kingdom	54
Plasma twister	56
I stand with my sister	58

The moon water trip	60
The Moon Country Bar & Museum	61
Morning news in the twenty-second century	63
Jacob as asteroid miner	65
Our day at the park	66
Al's Big Bang Grill	67
Dear Outer Space,	70
The moon tree in Central Park	72
The Planetary Invaders Recovery Group	73
Wild	74
An astronaut's daughter speaks	75
Blood in the cosmos	77
Alien breath	78
I walk into your galaxy	80
Gecko sex in space	82
Rejoice in caffeinated spin	83
Rejoice in erasure	84
Hello urban universe	85

Dear astronaut in training,

remember when you fixed
upon the rust world of Mars
through your boyhood window,

did you ever visualize
your fatherhood frame

would stand over
those north pole water molecules

that sit restrained
beneath the dust swirl surface?

You must know: water
thirty-five million miles away
cannot hold the same heft of home

as when you drink a tall glass
at the kitchen table
across from your son's preschool smile.

Open the front door. Mars
beams red within a blacktop darkness.

Once that rocket slices through the sky,
your son will learn
to say your name as a curse

while your ex sleeps solo
in the black hole of her mattress.

Three light-minutes away,
your Kansas lung sacs
will sweep in buttressed oxygen

over oxidized soil. Soil
a twin shade

of your father's rust-worn truck
engineless in your garage
a decade after his death.

The year before I left for Mars,

I cupped Kansas soil
in my harvest hands.

Now on Martian land,
skin-to-soil contact

is never authorized
as hominid microbes
would tarnish this crimson signature.

I am an alien five radio wave
minutes away
from your milk flow

where our son latches onto the globe
of your atmospheric breast
exposed in an autumn dawn.

Will we ever trade breaths again
like the month before I left for Mars,

we sat on the porch, fireflies'
supernovae popping alive

beneath the shield
of Earth's magnetic fist.

Within my white sheath spacesuit
in the openness of Arabia Terra,

solar radiation's sword
slices open my brain,

begins to collaspe the memory
of the cornhusk heartbeats
I left behind.

I must remember the lavender
petals strewn down our wedding aisle
back in my lava tube's shelter.

The day before I left for Mars,
I held our newborn
like a cup of water.

Fifty moons on,
his bones stretch

since I snapped his delivery
room photograph, cries

suspended
before my Kansas sight.

The cherry blossom planet

I swung by my ophthalmologist yesterday. She snapped a snapshot of my eyeballs laced in a pink permeation like that pink exoplanet reminiscent of a dark cherry blossom:

that's what a NASA astronomer said from his NASA highchair after he peered through a lens to watch the wobble of a mother sun as her blossom child recklessly spins like a teenager taking a swig of his father's gin. The fourteen year old broke the cabinet lock off, gawked into the clear liquid—*can I feel alive now?* shot through the chinatown of his brain

like a galactic courier coasting within a galactic hug. Her windshield shields the glare of maternal sunrays blanketing the cosmos with ultraviolet warmth. At the planet's precipice, the blossom clouds jettison her back, back to her father's Missouri garden

where his newlywed hands once planted a cherry seed just before the rains came with a clap.

My heartland moonbeams

I fish in my pocket,
pull out a Tubman
for another waxing gibbous rush
to spike into my prairie brain
right outside Wichita
where Lord's Diner
and that speed trap meet.
Samantha, smirking in her usual glow,
hands over my Heartland moonbeams
sloshing in a milk carton.

Brown bagging on I-35
through a chigger-heavy night,
I swallow swimming photons
born clean in The Sea of Serenity.
On an exit ramp, headlights whoosh by
as I guzzle stinging drops,
head swirling
at the intersection of host and desire
under the only sky
I will ever know.

The cosmos is alive

The Milky Way stretches
across a wheatland sky
as a screen door slaps shut.

A boy on the edge of manhood
walks out into a cloudless night.
In tall grass, he overhears
constellations narrate
their own mythology.

These storied stars
demand attention
from one boy

whose knees buckle
under a solar celebration
so much vaster than the brainwaves
of his God-imposed farmhand.

If he blinks behind his lens,
he'll miss the supernova burst
of Lyra's elephant stomp.

In a front porch stance,
his father demands
his son sit at the supper table,
pray to the Lord above.
After chewing down pot roast,

the son finds his own heaven
over a tray soaking photo paper
in a chemical ocean
where the Developer brings forth
a hymn of galactic sweep:

the cosmos is alive
through time-traveling shine
that bursts within
a photographic birth.

Are we alone?

On backyard grass
in morning dewdrop,

I scrawl *Are We Alone?*
on the paper I tie to Sally,
my homing pigeon, who vaults
into a blooming blue sky.

Back to my bedroom's
environment, I ask my mind:

is a denizen
of Proxima Centauri
lurking their telescopic vision
for a wavelength broadcast

flowing from Earth, from humanity,
from my divorced self's

atmospheric abandonment?
Through booming clouds,
Sally swoops to my ex's eyes, eyes
I still love.

Native

In the kick-my-teeth talk between space and gravity, my brain undulates against the rhythmic kick of Jupiter's spin tossing about orbiting oceans by the girth of her magnetic field. Within her Great Red Spot, I read *The Inferno* when your voice calls me home calls me home to a Europan hitchhiker staring back at me with those green binocular eyes as he swallows beef stew at our helium-based supper. I am native to this gas goliath named for the Roman god of thunder and sky. *Who are you?* to sit on the wood of my grandfather's chair. The foreigner immigrated from his ice-moon birth to the dense core of the solar system's closed fist where he rips out his eyeballs, plops them next to our whale-fat candle burning, and opens the screen door onto an atmospheric chainsaw.

I carry wonder

In the night's black crush,
I carry wonder

if we breathe alone
within our exhale of stars.

Under redshift hellos
scattered across this wide-armed sky,
how many atmospheres out there

welcome creatures
who breathe and talk of love.

Look up

On cold sand, waves smash
where we stand
trapped within
this San Francisco cityscape.

Look up. I bet our galactic road
curves to an Alpha
Centauri wedding
smacking upon lips of spectacle

but we cannot pierce
through streetlights
cloaking the starlight above.

We forgot how to shovel
Milky Way glow
into the grids of our minds.

Can we remember? Let's sprout
a new cosmic wonder.
Every star is a sun

my mother once said
back in the sponge
growth of my boyhood.

On our wedding night, remember
we sped across the Golden Gate
to delight upon a Sausalito sky
when you asked,

how many alien newlyweds
do you think are staring
at us in wonderment?

The Milky Way in L.A.

> Based on a true story

A blackout unlocks city-wide eyes.
In Echo Park, a man breathes a lost
panic on his walk home

as emergency dispatchers
brew their teas under the artillery
of voices phoning in
about a strange glowing cloud:

The Milky Way's detonated stars
drop onto Sunset Boulevard, disarming
the Hollywood glare bomb.

Three zip codes away
before their apartment window,
the man's family
gape at this shock in the sky
draped across a concrete sprawl.

Zoom in. The man, still trying
to get back to his bedroom,
slips on an unlit sidewalk.

Darkness watches him
flattened
under our galactic thumbprint
pressing down
on the neighborhood of his birth.

My steampunked universe

When I plop the universe down like a freshwater catch onto my kitchen counter, I shimmy in an engine piston now driving an expanding cylinder: the host to glass galaxies, cast-iron planets, lead marrow babies born screaming in super-Earth saloons. Back in the cosmic frontier, our ancestors shot spaceward long before I busted and barreled into an exomoon coal town with a forgotten name.

Watch a push of reptilian miners slither onto the company boxcar for the journey home to their sons and daughters hungry under oxygen-thin blankets. Watch as they wipe away soot from their scaled faces and blink in vivid vision through the unveiling of lips cheeks and eyes all fused to their family selves shining like a supernova—wait no—

like a Manhattan businessman, dripping from a midtown shower, he kisses his wife and peels away the skin of his suit a basketful of births after George Washington stands on the *island of many hills* to marry Martha and later reads aloud The Declaration of Independence before a 1776 crowd.

In a winter-slap darkness, patriots melt down a statue of King George III into 42,000 musket balls. Quick quick open your windows to hear our Brooklyn boys cracking gunpowder fire near The Red Lion Inn, red like Betelgeuse's solar headlight speeding through the steel-jointed dimensions of my steampunked universe.

My punked erasure

When I plop a freshwater ▮universe▮
down onto my kitchen counter ▮▮ I shimmy in an engine piston
▮ the host to glass ▮▮ ▮▮ ▮▮ planets ▮▮
▮ cast-iron galaxies ▮▮ a lead baby ▮▮ in a super-Earth
cosmic frontier ▮▮ ▮▮ ▮▮ ▮▮▮
▮▮ when our ancestors ▮▮ ▮ shot spaceward
▮▮ long after I barreled ▮▮ into an exotown
▮▮ ▮▮ with a foghorn name ▮▮ ▮▮▮

Watch a push of reptilians ▮▮ ▮▮ box ▮▮▮
in a slithering boxcar ▮▮ on the journey ▮▮ home ▮▮
▮▮ to their daughters and sons ▮▮▮
▮ hungry ▮▮ under ▮▮ oxygen ▮ thin blankets
Watch as they wipe ▮ away ▮▮ their sooty faces ▮
▮ and see ▮ in vivid ▮▮ vision
▮ through the ▮▮ unveiling ▮▮
of ▮ eyes ▮ lips ▮ and ▮ cheeks ▮ finding ▮ a ▮ fusion
▮ onto their family selves ▮▮ ▮

shining ▮ like a Manahatta man ▮ dripping from a ratty shower ▮
▮▮ he kisses his husband's ▮▮▮ mind ▮ ▮▮
▮▮▮ and peels away ▮▮▮ his skin suit ▮▮
a basketful of births ▮▮ ▮▮ after Martha marries Washington
▮▮ on the island of ▮▮▮▮ independent ▮ hills
▮▮ and later screams ▮▮▮ The Declaration
▮ ▮ ▮ before a '67 crowd ▮▮▮▮

In a punching darkness   patriots melt   down
         a statue   of Queen George
into 24,000 musket balls   Quick   quick
          open your   windows
to hear our womxn   cracking   fire
far from   The Red   Lion
like Betelgeuse's roaring head   speeding
through   the wild dimensions
              of my punked   universe

Ancient battle in the Nile

Born within Re's
heliocentric grip, Apopis
grew in a dim pocket of light
at the fringe of our solar system.

Once his orbit
pushes close to the sun,

his stone skin gets heated
into a serpentine dust tail
blazing upon a new
high-radiation flyby.

On the seventh hour
of every ancient Egyptian night,

Apopis slithered into the Nile,
sought to snap at Re
but Seth, a guardian
and master of disorder,

sliced the reptilian attack
with a spear.

Re's boat sailed on
into a neonate dawn
as Apopis hissed away,
bleeding in black water.

In his elliptical orbit,
the Serpent from the Nile

is still a transient traveler.
On April 13th, 2029, he will bite
the sight of stargazers
gazing up with their naked eyes.

Space vision

"On October 24, 1946, a V-2 was launched from the [White Sands] Missile Range while a mounted 35mm movie camera captured images . . . The grainy photo was . . . our first view of Earth from above the atmosphere."

We swapped out the war-
head for a camera
in a V-2 rocket that climbed
above the ocean talking
through the empty pockets
of clouds in unmapped atmosphere.

Beneath a black sweep
of gestating exploration,
our shutter winked
at Earth's curvature.

After the heat shield's return
to the desert sand, we soaked
photo paper. Over a tray, our eyes
dropped into a virgin sight
splayed on an ultrasound screen:

an unborn revealed
within humanity's womb.

Laika

Before her liftoff, Russian hands
chained the Moscow stray
within her cone-shaped coffin.
In Cold War galore,
newspapers swapped
between *Sputpup* & *Woofnik*
but we must shackle the puns

when the Control Room
sent a husky-terrier mix
to a barking incineration.
Seething calls overheated
the BBC switchboard: a Joan of Arc
burned up in the mesosphere, the chain
still locked to her forepaw.

Enos and Ham

> "After NASA launched Ham on a suborbital flight,
> Enos went into orbit in 1961."

On launch day, the Mercury capsule
malfunctioned
into a fisted-sun

with Enos the Chimp
restrained in the confined core.

As that hot steel prison
cut through the atmosphere
and swept twice around our Earth,

the lever that was built
to deliver a banana-
flavored treat

pulsated an electric shock
through his primate frame.
Enos got punished 76 times
for 76 right answers.

Ten months earlier, Ham the Chimp
shot to suborbital fame,
never leaving the sky's cerulean grip
yet he still splashed onto the cover of *Life*.

When Enos landed in hot
Bermuda waters, rescuers
pulled open the hatch

to spot a chimp
blinking within a spray of blood:
he ripped out every catheter
except the one in his heart.

We can all visit the bones
of "Ham: The First Astrochimp"
in America's capital

yet Enos' body is lost
as the first chimp
to reach orbiting speed.

Edwin's body

"His wife . . . never revealed what she did with his body . . .
For a memorial . . . look to . . . The Hubble Space Telescope."

Grace is driving. Grace is driving as she licks her lips. She licks her lips when a cerebral thrombosis imbues Edwin. A cerebral thrombosis imbues Edwin so she closes his eyes within the repose of a San Marino winter. A San Marino winter shivers their engine. Their engine shivers through a slapping rain. Through a slapping rain, Grace says *I Love You*. Grace says *I Love You* off a nowhere road. Off a nowhere road, she digs a devoted hole. She digs a devoted hole where Hollywood's glow never bleeds. Where Hollywood's glow never bleeds, Edwin's body seeps into soil. Edwin's body seeps into soil under stars buried behind black clouds.

Edwin's erasure

"His wife never revealed what she did with his body . . .
For a memorial . . look to . space."

      Grace licks her lips   when a cerebral thrombosis
           imbues Edwin   within the closed repose
             of a San Marino winter
    Their engine shivers   through a slapping rain
A nowhere rain says   *I Love You*   off a slapping road
        Grace digs   a glowing hole
   where Hollywood's devoted   never   bleed   out
      Edwin's body   seeps under stars
       dropped   behind black clouds

Project Echo

We gather as one nucleus
to fix sight upon a spectacle.

Minutes before at Wallops Island,
a NASA man released
a communications satellite

ballooning through the troposphere
where pressurized air expanded
until the silver shell ruptured.

At home, you smiled on our rotary dial,
you sat before our granulated television,
I listened to our radio

yet all three of us cluster
on the front lawn, eyes transfix

on a confetti of aluminum
sparkling in a Chesapeake sunset.

Planet X soap opera

Neighborhoods of rabbit ear
TVs picked up an exobroadcast
shoveling pixels

into American living rooms
flanked by apron-clad glee.

A Riverside wife went into
convulsions, a Newton priest
performed an exorcism

on his RCA, and a flat-earther
swam into the Atlantic,
seeking to breaststroke off the globe.

I dropped my jaw
like a milk carton, dairy spilled
before the plot points

of exoskeleton females
dramatizing within off-Nowhere theatrics.

At a scene's wrap, the production
cut to a commercial for extraterrestrial

body wash: a reptilian creature
lathered himself while reading off cue cards.

Suddenly, Walter Cronkite
discontinued the disturbance
to announce technical difficulties

into 1958 ears
while tongues wailed. Screams piped in
through my Wichita window

as I fashioned my remote
into a projectile at my screen,

mouth cranked open
to our solar system's data stream.

Survival

A cactus fruit bore little water
under the sun's mouth
that licked mean heat
onto your white tunic.

You swallowed a teaspoon of spit
kicked dry in that Nevada noon
with a waxing shine still hours away.

Trading in your tunic
for your spacesuit, you flew solo
over the moon's terrain.

Spacesuits must be white
because black is a hungry color
in celestial praise

where a rocket combustion
strung you over
a black lava bed
in lunar-locked shadow.

NASA spacesuit test

On my laptop screen, a Tumblr post
displays a 60s astronaut
standing sheathed
within a spacesuit's anonymity

before a camera. History opens:
when he waves quick
at the shutter, the orbit of his hand
blurs across the still-frame stirrings
of a man pressurized.

All the technicians see
is a cascade of white
like a dove flapping
through the sky's bruises.

Out my window, black clouds
inhale a view of our moon
separated by a light-second's divide

yet Earth's illuminated ally
has only shown one side
of her cratered visage
to you, me,

and the Space Race astronaut
resting on the floor
where he gathers a waxing glow
memory in his soft shell.

Pluto Time

"For just a moment near dawn and dusk each day,
the illumination on Earth matches that of high noon on Pluto."

In the glow of my laptop's light, I discover
my next Pluto Time: five minutes
before tomorrow's 6:26 sunrise,

the Berkeley dawn
birthing a new day
in the neighborhood of my c-section
will shimmer at the same strength

as Pluto's high noon sunlight
when weary photons
arrive gently
through a thin
methane and nitrogen atmosphere.

Let's not expect to spot
Gary Cooper's cowboy confidence
strutting under a red zenith sun
across the ice-shaped heart
of a most foreign world.

Out in the solar system's backcountry,
I'll finally lasso the time, lie back in a crater
with a western duel
enclosed inside a novel spine.

Yet just as fast, my solar
reading light
would perish from view
like an anointed planet
demoted to a dwarf orbit.

Tomorrow at 6:21 AM,
I'll haul my waking bones
into a crowning light
with a picture of Pluto's
heart in my hands.

The Apollo National Park

An earthrise arches along the horizon
as a summer worker
braces behind his register

before a California clan
arriving on the designer heels
of Gen X newlyweds.

They've all come
to open their wallets
under a heliocentric ascent

in a geodesic dome
designed to preserve lava root trees
for patrons to relish in alien air.

When the sun clicks into its zenith,
the worker uses his lunch break
to pay three Tubmans

for a 'One Small Step' sweatshirt
imported in from a sweatshop galaxy.
He wears his warmth

past a glass case
showcasing Armstrong's first footprint
that pulls capitalistic traffic

to the Apollo 11 module
where eyeballs latch
onto three seats of glory.

Lunar Trash Mission #7

> "As the Lunar Module Pilot for Apollo 16, [Charles] Duke . . .
> left a family portrait on the lunar surface."

On regolith ground, Sammy feeds
a whitewashed fifty-star flag
into metal teeth. The colonizers hired him
to wipe away the scape of Apollo praise.

The Apollo 16 module
requires a compactor's
clenched hand
to drop History down an open mouth.

For a breather in the Descartes Highlands,
Sammy gives serenity
to his heart chambers
with a big hug view
of our globe in half shadow.

There on a crest, Charles Duke
left a crinkled photograph:
Dottie in a sea-green dress; Thomas
with a hand on his mother's knee; Nicholas
still a boy in a tie and button-down;
Charles smiles in the skin of a family man

who's standing under a white crescent moon
stitched into the fabric
of a cerulean sky. As Sammy gazes
at this 1970s capsule, his daughter

cries along the 100th meridian
within his wife's arms
where she sings a melody
in their Kansas home.

Family land

Starlight swirls
inside my waxing sight
with redshift photons
stretched like skin

that fuse my family's
ancestral storybook

where a heroine of linked blood
sprints through the moon's spotlight
to do her own saving

in a corset. These pages
bound by epidermis
live on a wooden shelf

felled from a tree
older than my great-grandfather
who stood every night for 32 years
under a beckoning Berkshires sky

after he earned his bones
in World War I.

I occupy the same soil
his heels pressed into

when Maddy comes
to save me. Her devoted pupils
pour into my eyes
no longer coated by ancient stars.

Left to scream

As the Moon pulls a tide
onto my sandy feet,

I gawk upon the glow
gliding across the black ink sky

and wonder: how many brains
break into dementia fragments

up on the terrain
one light-second away?

Down on this beach, my brain's wave
flows back

to Grandpa Richard's Lewy Body.
His skinny skeleton

screams within hospice walls.
A bodiless scream

echoes through the predator
ocean between my ears.

In my future, will I become
the screamer?

If we spot life breathing
on the Moon, I'd seek to know

who gets treatment
within a mental health nexus

and who is left to scream
on an alien sidewalk

that mirrors
an American concrete block.

Moon rocks at large

> "The moon rock . . . was just one of about 180 moon rocks that are currently at large."

Snapshots of the moon rock got stamped onto milk cartons and pasted onto convenience store windows. Boston beat cops canvas underneath soda shop barstools—FBI agents bust down doors all Hollywood style—even my mother called in a tip, but it was just a piece of her cat's dried shit.

Last week as I drove with the windows down, I swear I saw a neighborhood father and son playing catch with one.

Once I pulled into the seclusion of home, Uncle John rang me up. He shot out *I just woke from a dream—or was it a nightmare?—where a Redcoat loaded his musket with a moon rock, and shot George Washington's left leg during The Siege of Boston. So you must look down the barrel of your eighteenth-century rusted musket.*

I did as I was commanded, but soon enough Sam started crying. As I bathed him in the kitchen sink, my mother unlocked my deadbolt to grab me by the collar and declare that *a sizable lot was buried beneath the black-eyed Susans in the bulls-eye of your garden.* I dug up the roots only to find the toil of diligence.

On a weekday night, I close the case file to swerve down Shawmut Avenue—I must get home to shepherd Sam asleep with the The Bryson Family Lullaby. Yet under the porch light, Maddy blankly states, *I just read to him a bedtime story.* In his nursery doorway, I see a fresh crib dream get snagged into a moonbeam's flow. Down at the dinner table, I know I'll need to replant fresh seeds before another Massachusetts winter freezes my soil and skin.

My cardiocentric sister

tasted kitchen salt,
spotted Sally's four-paw leap,
and heard the chime
of our grandfather clock
all through her heart's
sensory hustle.

One summer night
under a fresh strawberry moon
in our family's sleep submersion,
a ship singed our lawn
where a biped of triple helix fusion

scooped up her heart
and darted through an oxygen winter.
With captured alien booty,
humanzee hands
cracked open her rib slats.

The next morning's front page
declared a Martian Ma and Pa
extended their necks
over my sister's
chambers, her heart
once a hive of cognition.

Mary's moonbeams

On the Massachusetts coast,
they steamroll into a bustle
beside bakers and housewives

all clamoring for a spectacle
before 'The Diving Horse' show.

The animal splashes into a pool
as the father and son
walk toward The Big Top.

The father drops two Buffalo
nickels into a tin can,

lifts the son onto his shoulders.
They slice through the crowd's
ocean sweat. Up on a stage,

a pinstripe-suited man
jumps into the center. He is

here to tell you a story, a story I must say you shall never forget even after a thousand tomorrows. See you all must know the diamond clear lake only a stone's throw away. Well a decade past, I came upon a young woman standing at the lake's edge. The moon fired a fierce white as she stared into a beam's handprint pressed into the water. With my approach, her neck snapped up. After she nodded a calm greeting through the darkness, she collapsed into her captivation. When her soaking body crawled back onto land, oh the glow—my friends, I speak no lies—the glow infused the strength of our lunar sister's blaze into the tree trunks of her legs, the branches of her arms, the fruit of her sight. Dare to believe? Now you must. At long last ladies and gentlemen—please brace yourselves—I give you Mary's moonbeams

busting out
into her ball of blindness
like a locomotive headlight

shoving darkness
into the timeout corner.

Lunar Kingdom

What a sight to spy
on a father squeezing his family
into one space-car spot.

Any townie will insist
>*You can't miss Lunar Kingdom.*
>*They built it right off the Lunar Maria Highway*
>*in an impact crater.*

Just beyond the last row of engines,
give attention
to a retiree rocking on her front porch.

The woman gazes through glazed eyes
at our principal players
bustling through the turnstile
before an eruption of customers

shoves them to an ice cream stand
>*'Proudly Serving Brighams'*
A scooper sprinkles on
a handful of jimmies.

>*On the house sweetcheeks*
but this father
doesn't take any winking charity.

He slaps down a Stowe
while the wife and two sons frog-lick
in The Armstrong Walk line
that bisects blacktop slather.

With their bodies
bushwhacked by sunlight, focus
on the father's mouth

mouthing *fuck you*
with unwashed words
when he herds three characters
to a restaurant chill.

Plasma twister

I cannot forgot our walls,
our doorframe, our baby room
a radiant Grandpa Charlie built
as newscasters swarm in like cicadas
to record the neighborhood's
beaten homes and bleeding faces
feeding back to tornado alley earthlings
swatting at the power button.
Back to you, Suzanne. Thank you, Larry.
Let's check in with our five-day forecast.
Knees buckle. I shake on the curb.
Blink blink but I won't look
at rigor mortis along the cul-de-sac's
curved spine. After Charlie
crumples onto the ground, a camera
snatches up his grief for viewing blinks.
Sue from three addresses down
rushes over cables
slinking across bloody ground.
She clutches her daughter's
school photo. *Suzzy, Suzzy,*
ah Jesus—have you seen my daughter?
I manage to utter   *no.*
Here is where I once pushed
a laughing Sam on his swing.
A reporter calls me over
to stand with a straight back.
Live from Solar Town,
these roots once dug
into photospheric depths.
She holds the microphone before my mouth:
When we first immigrated here,

*Nan Bryson planted a lemon tree here
but she was killed in her sleep
as the twister ripped everything away.*
She nods, thoughtfulness glazed on.
So touching, mamn. Your heart must break.
I stare into the red blinking light,
agree with a quiet   *yes.*

I stand with my sister

in the shell of our ex-living room.
Our Solar Town neighbor
gets shot by a camera's gun
for earthly tv eyes.
We stumble among
our patched quilts, roof tiles,
blood splayed across uprooted lawns.
No serenity here
after a twister ripped away the only home
our breaths belong in.
On the photospheric
cold spot we immigrated to,
we must remember how Grandpa
fused four walls and a roof
onto this fusion ball.
Just one sleep ago, Maddy
sat in Charlie's handcrafted chair
and I swallowed
Nan's banana nut bread
within our private haven.

By Maddy's side, my footfalls

move onto the cul-de-sac

splintered into slashes

where plasma seeps through concrete.

With sweat beads gathered across my brow,

I pull out a Bryson handkerchief

from my breast pocket.

In the cotton center, I feel our family

crest once stitched

by Nan's weathered hands.

The moon water trip

Dusk coats the parched topography as I grab a bucket and shovel to drive my Plymouth through The Vallis Alpes Valley that once flowed along a river's lava curve.

Fast-forward to the solidification of now, a throng of schoolchildren walk across the walkway. Once I speed ahead to the cold trap craters strewn across the north pole, I slip on a sweater— *Jacob! You'll get sick in that -400° chill!* —

and kick up a plume of billion-year-old regolith. Minus an atmospheric shield, dust takes flight into a black sweep like the paper airplane Sam once snapped over a high tide at Revere Beach.

Under a mountain of constellations, I dig and sweat in the glow of my headlights. When my shovel finally gives way, I bend down to splash the familiar across my face—like a Frog Pond awakening under a ruthless Boston sun—but I must gather myself as the man I am. Breathe now. The shadow divide jolts my eyes,

a beauty I cannot pocket while I kiss Maddy's strained face, wolf down a pot roast, and hand over the sloshing delivery in the morning. At my office window, I light a smoke before the skyline burning this roasted-particle land.

The Moon Country Bar & Museum

When Buzz put his B&B Bar
in Armstrongville up for sale,
I propped a lien on my home
to snatch the building.

Now I showcase the organs
of yesterday to liquored patrons.
On permanent display,
a cattle rancher's rope
encircles a bullet in the far wall.

I'll run my thumbprint over the metal
while I picture Marshall Raymond Lewis
collapsing onto the cigarette-strewn floor
after a fast finger got the first shot off.

History lost the outlaw's face
but we know he fled south
past the Apollo 11 landing site.

Charlie joined a posse who fed
their rabbit-hunting dachshunds
meat scraps, loaded their Winchester M183s
to search for The No-Name
in The Shackleton Impact Zone,
our blue globe hanging in the backdrop.

Buzz greeted the renegades'
victory return
by pouring a free shot
of Tanglefoot whiskey
for every dry throat. Charlie's whiskey
sting is still family memory.

I flip over the 'Open' sign,
wait for customers to step
through those batwing doors.
At the workweek's end,
my eyes often find themselves
staring into the barrel

of a five-shot Paterson revolver.
Later, my hands rediscover
the notches in the bar's
carefully preserved surface.

Morning news in the twenty-second century

My father kills a fly with the comics,
returns to his front page spread

as I gape over my mug's milk swirl
pushing within black pressure.

At the round kitchen table,
we chew scrambled eggs
dipped in ketchup, our teeth

stained red by the soil
infusing our meals.

*They burned the leader
of that uprising*

to ashes, he says, a fact
in the mirrored tone
of the day's forecast.

I have to speak with a stab,
*but they can't burn what she means
to the people still alive.*

My father sends out a cackle
that stomps out to the Mars-

evolved tomato garden
listening through slave-watered growth.

These red globes buckle at the arrival
of his mocking sound wave.

I leave my dirty plate in the sink
to watch through the bars
of my bedroom window

the uprisers return as a line of bodies
pick ripe roundness
seeded in lucrative land.

From his watchful shade, the master
bites into a slice

screaming against the grind
of suppression.

Jacob as asteroid miner

We landed on an orbiting body
christened to honor
the long-dead deity
of home and hearth.

The mine, the saloon,
the schoolhouse: all visible
from our new home.

Over a Vestan year,
you rose with the droves
before you descended

into the black soup of pursuit,
one among a swath
schlepped down an elevator shaft.

At dusk, the screen door
swung wide upon your return,
that frostbite breeze
cooling my Irish stew.

With your face blackened
by iron-rich clay, you wiped away
soot from your eyelids

and doled out a passing kiss,
squeezing our supermarket survival
into my breast pocket.

Under a wraparound glare,
you threw your jeans
onto our bedroom floor.

Our day at the park

My brain vibrates with family chatter as we feed our four bodies into the mouth of a snake line. *We should have got here earlier,* you say with a snark. *Well you didn't calm Sam from another nightmare and make Sunday pancakes this morning.* The children bounce as expensive springs who reach euphoria before The Vestan Amusement Park's commerce cascade. They tug from both sides at my azure-sky shirt with demands for their own stuffed earthly animal, but I simply survey a ferris wheel's cyclical circumference, a four-seat boat floating through some constructed dark passage, and a merry-go-round where creatures of mythos are static with poles forced through artifical frames. With the Stowes and Tubmans snug in my wallet, I paid for 2 adults and 2 children to partake in the prospect of elation on this 4.4 billion-year-old asteroid. Willing human screams gather velocity on spinning rides bolted into the rock we walk across to find a map from a kiosk display. You reach for the navigation but I swat you away like a housefly. *I got this. You just enjoy this day.* I lead us to the boat ride. Once Sam and David spring onto wood, I step on while I reach back for your hand yet I'm only greeted by fleshless space. You retreat to the testosterone injection you'll receive at a roller coaster's climax. *Where did daddy go? He needs some air,* I say to our genetic shadows. We're carried across a water flow like the universe waving hello.

Al's Big Bang Grill

When I moved with my children through a wormhole into a new neighborhood, I sat in Al's Big Bang Grill where I swallowed a lager and salviated over Al's signature hamburger alongside my new neighbors.

*

After I leave the police station at every workday's end, I'll curse God within a traffic pack for conversation and a simple slice of cherry pie. If you wish, I'll recite the menu like Gospel.

As I sleep, grease fumes seep into my bed sheets, my Rottweiler, my thumbprint.

*

On the loading dock, an eighteen-wheeler arrives from the Fourth Dimension to dump off clothing and glassware. If I need a space to escape, I'll visualize green hands gathering the cotton for a rich customer's shirt.

*

I gave up on finding a window view during The Hydra Supernova: tourists crunched up against the glass with their cameras, chattering *Did you? Can you?* snap a sharable capsule of another time-bomb death.

*

Once I toss my badge and .38 on the dresser (a snapshot of Maddy in framed display), I stand still as if my clock hands are in rigor mortis though in truth the cashier's *DING* just ceased invading. Al turned off his fryer, tallied his money, waved bye for now to the temple of his kitchen.

Through a glass pane separation, he veers past on his way home to read his daughter a story like the ritual I once shared with Sam where he held rapture over an alien world only accessed through a wardrobe.

Dear Outer Space,

Do you go by *Miss* or *Mrs?*
If we become cordial,
will you take *Hey Outer?*

You must know galaxies gossip
how the Laniakea Supercluster
unlawfully branches
across the hem of your skirt

but no one voices
that your cartilage is a dead relic
after 13.82 billion cycles
of rising from a gas bed

to that steel-floor factory.
You clock-in to pipe
the unity of spacetime into our universe
for a slim wage and no pension.

To meet quota, your body
spawns another super-Earth.

Do you dare assembly line a desire
to find Escape where no one
will throw you a hooked stare.

Once you land on a future world,
you'll exhale a genesis breath
into an atmosphere that will never
slaughter a Miss or Mrs.

Hey Outer, how do you know
you'll find your friend Escape?

For now, this is your existence
at another workweek's end:
trudge home to fried dark energy

washed down with a subatomic brew,
bubbles bullying down
your throat's black star alley

when your mother calls
to wish you a happy birthday. She sings
into the phone as you begin to cry.

The moon tree in Central Park

> "Apollo 14 launched . . . Stuart Roosa . . . orbited above in the command module. Packed . . . were hundreds of tree seeds . . . the resulting seedlings were planted throughout" America.

I once overheard hot Brooklyn talk: a moon-traveling sweetgum seed found a home in Central Park among the roots fixed to forested ground.

As I barreled down an afternoon trail, I swiveled my head into an enchantment before a swathe of light glowing from the sweetgum's trunk to branches

while the leaves' green growth was still lassoed in shadow like an impact crater too deep to sunbathe in—like a tourist stretched out on Brighton Beach sand—like a Little Italy baker stretching and rolling her dough into loaves—like my bike rolling down to that shitty bodega at Flushing & Bushwick.

I drank a 40 after I found a moon tree today. What have you accomplished?

With an autumn dawn knocking, I returned with a buzz to my sweetgum haven where I found the ghost of her *Houston To Mission Control* past still bursting back—can you see, yes can you see the bark of this tree smiling moonbeams into Central Park vegetation like our radio waves careening into lunar ears.

The Planetary Invaders Recovery Group

In the north end of Bushwick, we gather in the Y basement where I sequester my reptilian body from all the mammals to hock a venomous loogie at the monkeys cleaning each other.

On a cheap metal chair within claw's reach of the fire alarm, I sit with my kind, old allies like the mutated chameleons Gary and Rose who just got hitched after they squashed those Neptunians from some floating cloud existence.

Fifty heartbeats in, I gladly fall into a trance: what if my four-fingered claw pulls the switch, steals wheels to Pluto still ripe for spearing the native inhabitants. I can see, can you see blood smearing across a galleria of domination?

I wiped out the Europans last weekend after I drilled through the ice and sucked up those sea creatures with a bendy straw.

Back in the bitch of a Brooklyn winter, they confiscated my straw, plopped my green brain here before a programmed machine: *Did your parents label you as evil? Did you invade sand castles, tree houses, bungalows as a boy? When did this desire start?* I was born with sharp claws.

One-hundred heartbeats in, I trip into submission when my friend Helen, a black python, begins her confession of failed conquest.

Pluto must wait until the next solar eclipse: the humans will burn their eyes out while I slip away like an unseen fish finning through a depth waiting to be hunted.

Wild

The coast-to-coast news
just broadcasted a Martian radio wave
shouting an encroaching invasion.

You call Pastor Paul to ask,
*should we uphold the faithful
structure of violence?*
Over the landline, he commands that
these aliens are not God's creatures.

Out in the barn, mother feeds
the chickens as the wild donkey
I call Beacon
slams her head into our locked gate.
She saw her first human last Sunday.

When the galactic foreigners
step / crawl / slither
off their light-speed ship
onto the prairie of my youth,

will we slaughter upfront
or tame their brains
by slapping neurological expansion
into submission.

With your shotgun finger
ready to squeeze, you shout
GET AWAY SON!
from your double-barrel power.

I must watch your shotgun kickback
execute Beacon
who broke the lock
and rammed her body
through our kitchen window.

An astronaut's daughter speaks

This supermoon sky
mirrors the rot
beneath the floorboards
of your ex-living room

where Mom counts her diner tips.
Is there enough for dinner?

On the front yard, weeds
spike out all around. Up up.
I glare at toss-away stars

poisoned since you left
Denver's city burn
leaking into my 1-25 horizon.

Last Sunday, I dreamed
the ruthless universe
spearheaded your silver-plated spacecraft
through a wormhole

to an alien's face.
How many noses, mouths, brains?
I of course have one of each

as I walk back inside.
In the kitchen window frame,
Mom returns holding eggs
to fry yellow sun yolks.

We sit at the table,
our family gathering of two.
If you return, will I greet a hero
or a skeleton in a suit?

You must understand: when I speak
of we, I no longer include you
beyond the biology I'm bound to.

Blood in the cosmos

I got a sticker at the blood center
for giving away eight pints
over a year: O positive
disbursed into alien veins
yet can I call them aliens
when my hemoglobins
flows through consciousness
of human cognition.

Free of headlight stain
along a farmland road,
I look upon the cosmos
like a body sliced open
by my eye of precision
asking   *are we alone?*
under constellations I praise.

At home with a flickering bulb,
I stick my sticker
on the lampshade
and play "The Golden Record"
bolted onto Voyager I
now beeping through interstellar space.
Blind Willie Johnson sings here
is mute there
on his way to alien ears.

Alien breath

A July morning screams hello.
On my doorstep,
twenty-first century radiation

assaults the hominid skin
stretched across my bones.

Last night, under a patch of unspoiled sky
on an Oakland Hills street
where I claim residence and heartbeats,

I gaped upon a confetti of starlight
that pierced atmospheric density.

I stowed this sharpness
within the zip code cones
of my 946-double-1 eyes.

As I step on cracked concrete,
cars swerve by

like Earth jettisoning through
the solar system's spacetime homeland.

Our Stars and Bars homeland
is stretched to breaking

over who has an authority knee
pressed to their neck
yesterday, today or tomorrow.

On rocky worlds
beyond any rocket's reach,
which aliens can't breathe?

When one breath is lost,
who brands rigor mortis
as a misplaced heartbeat?

The bones in a foreign graveyard
cannot protest alone

like American skulls
covered with black soil.

I walk into your galaxy

where I promptly trip
on some cracked dark matter.

Red whiskey-eyed giants
bicker on their Welcome Home mats
over my alien plasma

blazing past the community garden
of Big Bang care.

Dishes in the sink, you drag
yourself to the Photon Refinery,
pull a double shift

after the Fourth Dimension
gossiped at the Crab Nebula's

baby shower
about the tuition bill you pay
for your gravity-expanding daughter

at The Horsehead Stellar Nursery.
Helium even added

how your hothead firstborn
must rock to sleep in the pricey
'Crib of Consciousness.'

Down into the bush league
of your blackstone town,

you ripped away one month's pay
for the scenic mattress and lumber
schlepped to your doorstep

with a flag waving
on your lawn. I'm waving back
at your photospheric shutters

before I hook one block over
to buy a high-proof handle

from a cashier burning hydrogen
under his leather skin.

At last, I pulsate
along a interstellar avenue
towards the galactic exit.

Gecko sex in space

I'm a space gecko. I'm a space gecko
spinning in the intimacy

of freefall copulation. What? Yes,
my shell must gestate, my shell

must form a squamatic daughter
without the bother

of an atmospheric sweep of strength.
If her birthplace

is unbound from Earth,
is her birth brain

extraterrestrial?
Anton strides over

to gape at a failure of bones:
he fails to spot the split fork

of his ancestors' skeleton structure.
So we toss our spawn, a reject

of misshapen proportion,
into the airlock.

Outer Space has her way
as we slap our tails

and go missionary
into the morning.

Rejoice in caffeinated spin

The ISS hugs the Earth above an electric sprawl that pulsates into the bliss of you sipping a zero-g espresso with praise to the crema seized in pleasure on your tongue as rejuvenated by the beans who delivers a concentrated punch across the basin of your brain—rejoice before the milk and the sun while our mother slurps her morning tea—burnt mouth within the atmosphere where your Armstrong action figure stands on a shelf: the black visor cloaks the oxygenated replica into a faceless star.

Rejoice in erasure

The ISS hugs ~~the Earth above~~ an electric sprawl that pulsates into ~~the bliss of~~ you sipping a zero-g espresso with ~~praise to the~~ crema seized ~~in pleasure~~ on your tongue as ~~rejuvenated by the~~ beans ~~who~~ deliver~~s~~ a concentrated ~~punch across the basin of your~~ brain—~~rejoice~~ within the Milky Way ~~and the sun~~ while our mother's ~~slurps her morning tea~~ —mouth burns within the atmosphere where your Armstrong action figure ~~on a shelf: the black visor cloaks the~~ stands as a oxygenated replica into a full-faced~~less~~ sun.

Hello urban universe

In a blackout darkness, my mother beats
an egg within a lunar glow
swelling on her counter.
As I sit at the supper table
before a scrambled hill,

I need an escape. At 4th and Clement,
Blue Danube Coffee House
where I love to write stanzas
locked their door. Where can I go?

The Milky Way
pulsates across this San Francisco sky.
There must be a book
on an urbanite's proper etiquette
if they greet foreign shine
for the first time

but I'm beckoned now
to Golden Gate Park's
verdant envelopment. Look up.
Orion's Belt buckles onto sawtoothed
Spanish chestnut leaves.

Even among flora I know
as my friends, I'm lost
under a swath of strange stars
beaming
onto my California body.

Notes

"Hello Universe Lovers": Apopis (the Serpent From the Nile) was the ancient Egyptian deity for chaos; Ra was the ancient Egyptian sun god.
The Editors of Encyclopedia Britannica. "Apopis: Egyptian God." Britannica.com. Last updated: 12 January 2023.

"Space Vision": Major, Jason. "This Is The Very First Photo of Earth From Space." *Universe Today*. 23 December 2014.

"Laika": "The She-Hound of Heaven." *Time*. 18 November 1957. 33.

"The Press: Dog Story." *Time*. 18 November 1957.

"Enos and Ham": Kelvey, Jon. "60 Years Ago, A Space Chimpanzee Made History—And Left A Dark Legacy." *Inverse*. 29 November 2021.

Schierkolk, Andrea. "HAM: The First Astrochimp." *The Micrograph*. 26 September 2019.

"Edwin's Body": Bryson, Bill. *A Short History of Nearly Everything*. Broadway Books. 2004. 132.

"Project Echo": "The Odyssey of Project Echo." NASA.gov. 27 October 2016.

"NASA Spacesuit Test": *Magic Transistor*. Tumblr.

"Pluto Time": "Find Your Pluto Time." Solarsystem.nasa.gov. Last updated: 5 December 2017.

"Lunar Trash Mission #7": "The First and Only Family Photo on the Moon." Twisted Sifter. 22 October 2017.

"The Year Before I Left for Mars": After "Before I Left for Mars" by Margaret Rhee.

"My Steampunked Universe": Manhattan (original name is Manahatta) likely originates from the Lenape language word Mannahatta with a meaning "island of many hills."

Holloway, Marguerite. "URBAN TACTICS; I'll Take Mannahatta." *The New York Times*. 16 May 2004.

"Moon Rocks at Large": "Ark. Archivist Finds Missing Moon Rock." *NPR*. 26 September 2011.

"The Moon Tree in Central Park": Dr. Williams, David R. "The Moon Trees." Nssdc.gsfc.nasa.gov. Last updated: 16 December 2022.

"Gecko Sex in Space": Deng, Boer. "The Sad Conclusion to the Tale of the Sex Geckos Lost in Space." *Slate*. 2 September 2014.

About the Author

In Oakland, California, Keith Gaboury is a preschool teacher by day and a poet by night. His poems have appeared in such literary publications as *Poetry Quarterly, New Millennium Writings,* and *The San Francisco Public Library Poem of the Day Series.* He has chapbooks from *Duck Lake Books, The Pedestrian Press,* and *Finishing Line Press.* A full-length poetry collection is forthcoming from *Falkenberg Press.* Keith is also the president of the Berkeley Branch of the California Writers Club.

Learn more at:
keithmgaboury.com

www.ingramcontent.com/pod-product-compliance
Lightning Source LLC
Chambersburg PA
CBHW070937160426
43193CB00011B/1723